Exploring Space

Lesley Sims

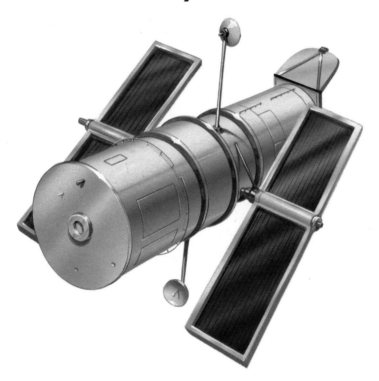

Watts Books
London • New York • Sydney

© 1993 Watts Books

Watts Books
96 Leonard Street
London EC2A 4RH

Franklin Watts Australia
14 Mars Road
Lane Cove
NSW 2066

UK ISBN: 0 7496 1032 8

10 9 8 7 6 5 4 3 2 1

Series editor: Pippa Pollard
Editor: Felicity Trotman
Design: Shaun Barlow
Cover design: Edward Kinsey
Artwork: Jamie Medlin
Cover artwork: Hugh Dixon
Picture research: Ambreen Husain

Educational advisor: Joy Richardson

A CIP catalogue record for this book
is available from the British Library

Printed in Italy by G. Canale & C. SpA

Contents

What is space?

The Earth is surrounded by an invisible layer of air. This is the **atmosphere.** We could not breathe without it. Space is everything which lies beyond the atmosphere. It is made up of thousands of millions of galaxies with nothing in between them. Inside the galaxies are stars, planets and moons.

▽ We live in a spiral galaxy, like this one.

Astronomy

Astronomy is the study of space. People who spend their lives observing and finding out about galaxies, stars, planets and moons are astronomers. They use **telescopes** to observe the sky. Telescopes are housed in observatories. For centuries, astronomers could only study from Earth. Even the largest telescopes did not show them very much.

▽ An early telescope.

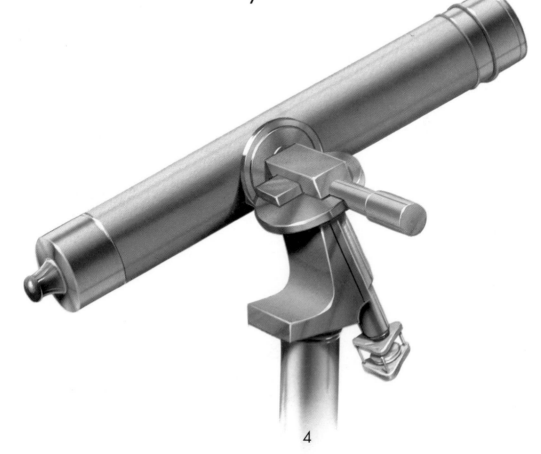

▷ Making a mirror for a modern telescope.

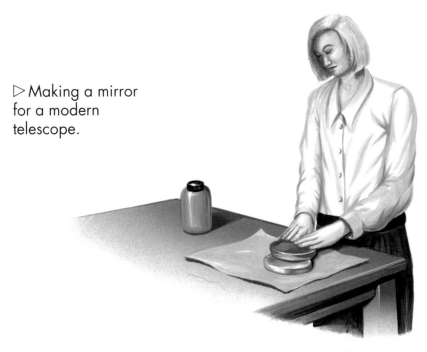

▽ The domed roof of this observatory opens to let the telescope see the sky.

Into the sky

To learn more, astronomers had to go into space. **Rockets** were built to carry **spacecraft** to explore the stars and planets. They have to be powerful enough to escape the pull of the Earth's **gravity.** A rocket works by **propulsion.** Its engines burn fuel which makes hot gas. As the gas is forced out of the rocket, it is pushed along.

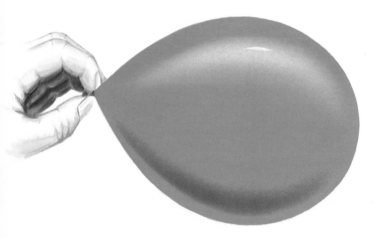

△ If you blow up a balloon and then let it go, it will fly. The balloon is pushed along by the force of the air leaving it.

▷ This is one of the earliest rockets. It only flew 12 metres into the air.

▽ A rocket being launched into space.

Humans in space

In 1957 the Soviets launched Sputnik 1. It was the first man-made object sent into space. Four years later, Yuri Gagarin became the first human in space. He **orbited** the Earth once. The **astronaut** Alan Shepard was the first American in space. They showed that people could survive space travel. Later, Soviet and American astronauts walked in space.

▽ Sputnik 1 carried a radio. Scientists could follow the signals it broadcast as Sputnik orbited the Earth.

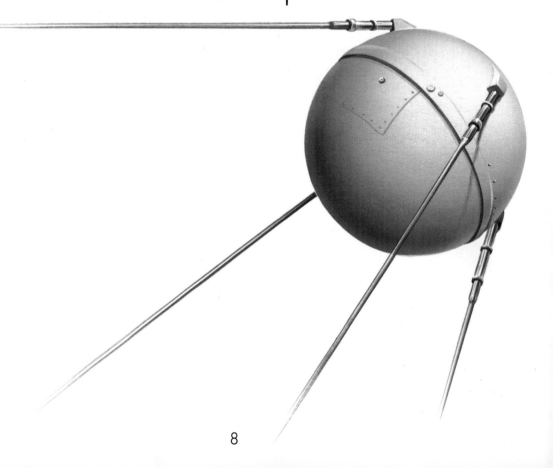

▷ Yuri Gagarin's spaceship was called Vostok 1.

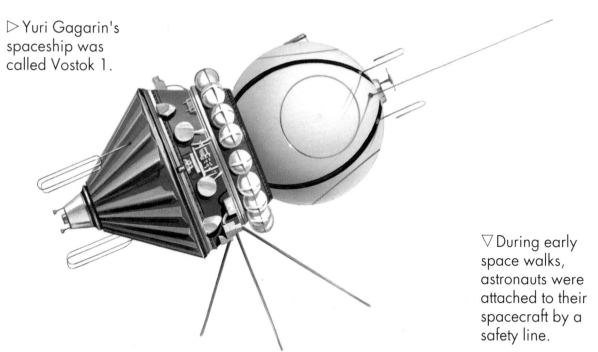

▽ During early space walks, astronauts were attached to their spacecraft by a safety line.

Saturn rockets

The next challenge was to send a human to the Moon. The Americans built the rocket Saturn 5 to **launch** their spacecraft **Apollo.** It split into three parts, called **stages.** The first pushed the rocket into the sky. Then it ran out of fuel and fell to the Earth. The second stage took over. Saturn's speed increased. The third stage took Apollo into space.

▽ The Saturn rocket was so powerful and noisy, it shook buildings many kilometres away.

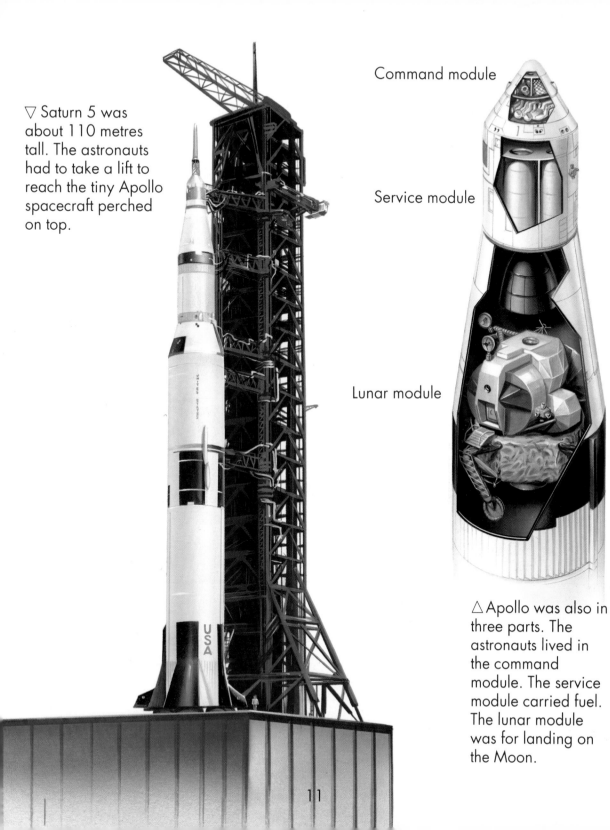

Command module

Service module

Lunar module

▽ Saturn 5 was about 110 metres tall. The astronauts had to take a lift to reach the tiny Apollo spacecraft perched on top.

△ Apollo was also in three parts. The astronauts lived in the command module. The service module carried fuel. The lunar module was for landing on the Moon.

On the Moon

On 20th July 1969, the lunar module from Apollo 11 landed on the Moon. Neil Armstrong became the first human to walk on the Moon. Five other Apollo **missions** have visited the Moon since then. Astronauts explored the surface of the Moon in a buggy called a Lunar Rover. They brought back over 380 kilos of Moon rock for scientists to study.

▽ Setting up an experiment on the Moon.

◁ When the last astronauts left the Moon in 1972, they left behind their space buggy. It will still be there today.

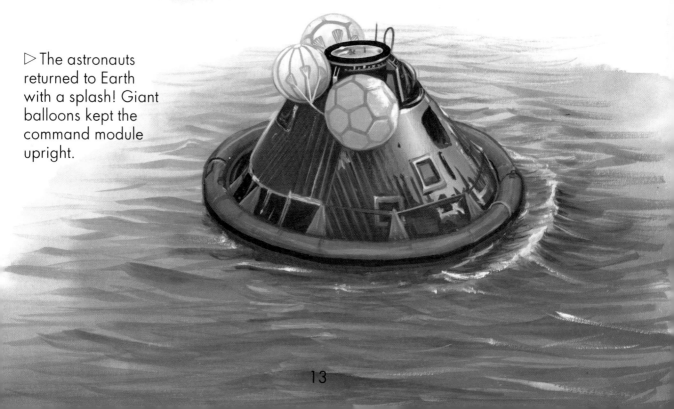

▷ The astronauts returned to Earth with a splash! Giant balloons kept the command module upright.

The space shuttle

▷ The launch of the first shuttle, Columbia, in April 1981.

Only one-thirtieth part of each massive Saturn 5 ever returned to Earth. A new rocket was needed for every flight. It was a very expensive way to visit space, so the shuttle was developed. This is a spacecraft which can be used many times. It looks like an aeroplane stuck to the side of a rocket. It is launched like a rocket, but lands like a glider.

▷ Inside a shuttle. Below the flight deck are the crew's living quarters.

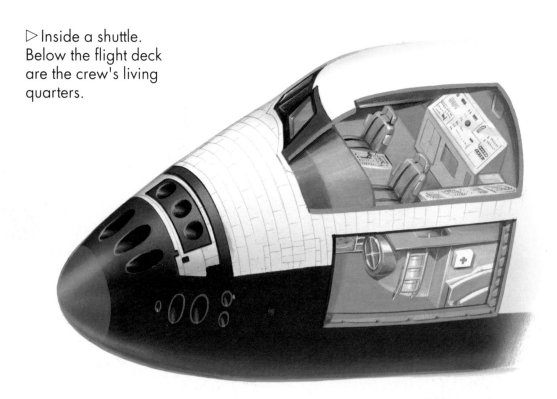

A shuttle flight

Two minutes after launch, the solid rocket boosters fall to Earth. Six minutes later, the fuel tank is abandoned to fall through the atmosphere, where it burns up. The shuttle goes into orbit around the Earth. When the astronauts are ready to return, the shuttle's engines fire to take it out of orbit. As it re-enters the Earth's atmosphere, the shuttle glows red-hot.

▽ The rocket boosters are recovered and can be used again.

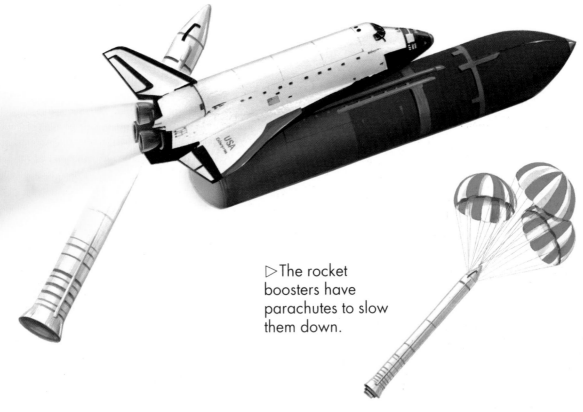

▷ The rocket boosters have parachutes to slow them down.

▷ The outside of the shuttle is covered in thousands of tiles to protect it from the atmosphere.

▽ The shuttle glides noisily to Earth without power, so the astronauts have to make a perfect landing first time.

The space station

Unlike the shuttle, a space station remains in orbit around the Earth. Shuttles bring supplies of air, food and water from the Earth. From the station, the crew can study the Earth and space. They can see if a long stay in space harms the human body. In one experiment, they made special metals and crystals for computers.

▷ America plans to put a space station into orbit in the 1990s. It will be taken in pieces on the shuttle and put together in space.

▷ The Soviet space station Mir. It is much more spacious than a shuttle.

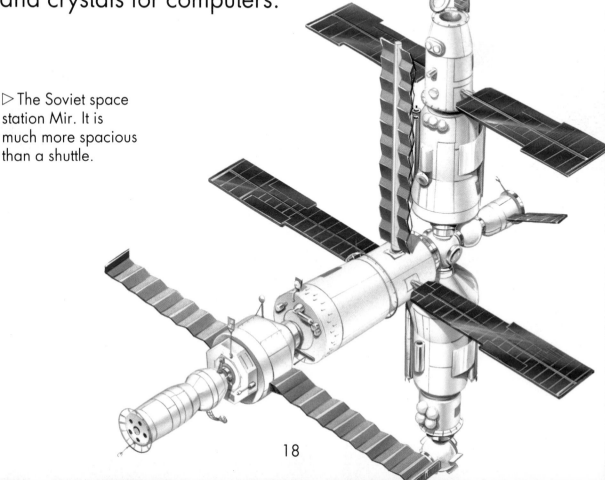

Living and working in space

There is no gravity in space, so everything floats. Inside the shuttle or space station the crew push themselves around. Their food is sticky to keep it on the plates. When the crew are working inside, they wear ordinary clothes. When they go outside to carry out repairs, they wear a suit as protection from the extreme temperatures and dust.

▷ The astronauts use gas-powered back-packs to move around.

▽ This astronaut is holding her food to stop it floating away.

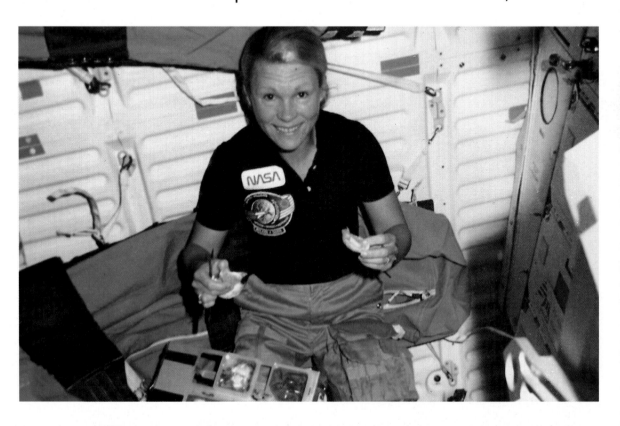

Satellites

A **satellite** is an object which orbits another. The Moon is a natural satellite of the Earth. There are thousands of man-made satellites orbiting the Earth. At first they were launched by rockets. Now they are taken into space by the shuttle. Satellites have solar panels. They use the light of the Sun to make electricity. When they are in shadow, they use batteries.

▽ Satellites are delicate. They are built in special, clean rooms. Even a tiny speck of dust can damage them.

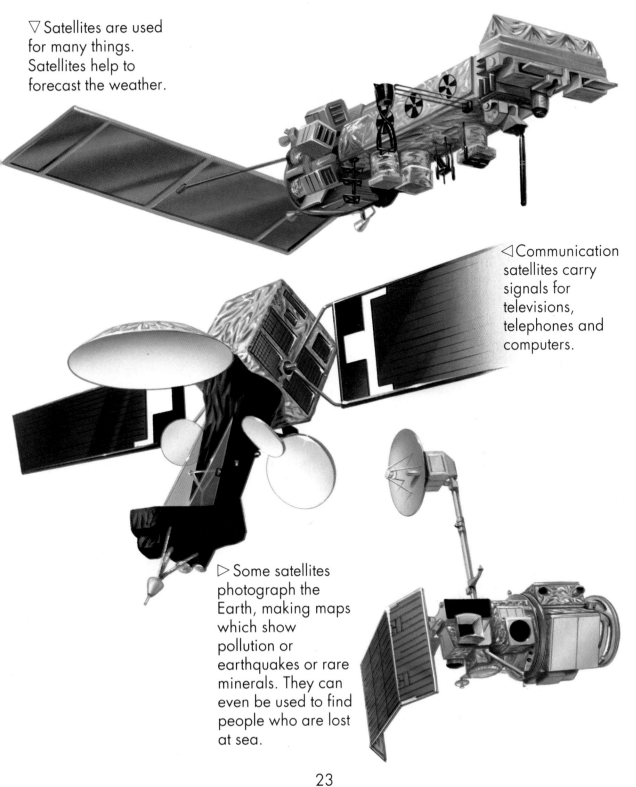

▽ Satellites are used for many things. Satellites help to forecast the weather.

◁ Communication satellites carry signals for televisions, telephones and computers.

▷ Some satellites photograph the Earth, making maps which show pollution or earthquakes or rare minerals. They can even be used to find people who are lost at sea.

23

Space probes

▷ A close-up of Jupiter taken by Voyager 2.

Probes are robot explorers, sent into space to investigate distant planets and moons. Probes have landed on Venus and Mars. Voyager 2 went on a 12 year journey to fly past four of the outer planets – Jupiter, Saturn, Uranus and Neptune. The first probes to visit the outer planets were Pioneers 10 and 11.

△ The probe Giotto travelled into Halley's Comet.

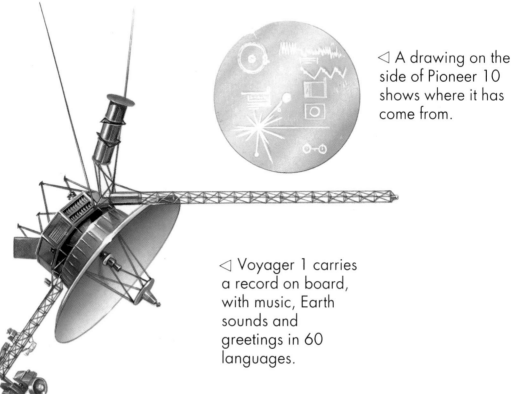

◁ A drawing on the side of Pioneer 10 shows where it has come from.

◁ Voyager 1 carries a record on board, with music, Earth sounds and greetings in 60 languages.

Galileo and Hubble

The space probe Galileo was launched in 1989. It will spend two years studying Jupiter when it finally arrives. The Hubble Space Telescope went into orbit in 1990. Hubble can see seven times further into space than other telescopes. Hubble's first pictures showed that something was wrong with the telescope. Astronauts will be sent in the shuttle to mend it, in 1993.

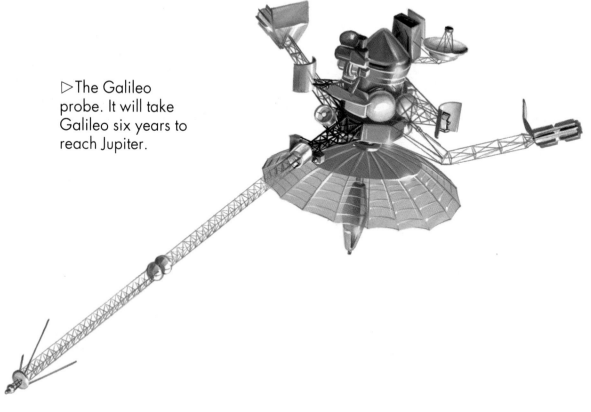

▷ The Galileo probe. It will take Galileo six years to reach Jupiter.

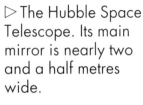
▷ The Hubble Space Telescope. Its main mirror is nearly two and a half metres wide.

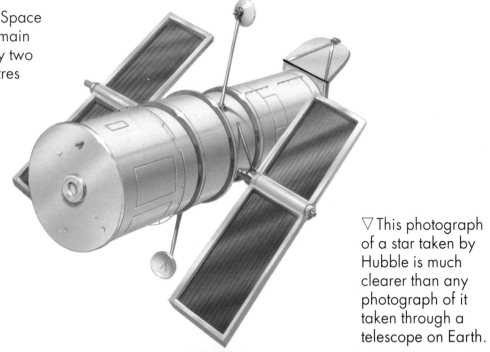

▽ This photograph of a star taken by Hubble is much clearer than any photograph of it taken through a telescope on Earth.

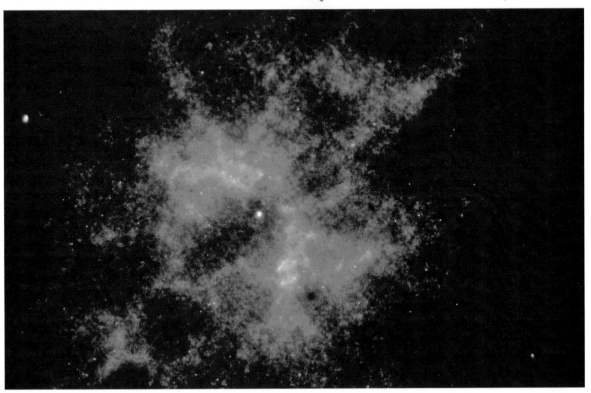

Space in the future

When countries began sending rockets and satellites into space, they raced each other to see who could be first. Now they help each other and work together. Scientists from many countries plan to build the space station Freedom. In 1997, the international satellite Columbus will be launched to observe the Earth.

▷ America hopes to build a permanent base on the Moon, where people can live and work. It may look like this.

▽ American and Soviet astronauts meeting in space when their Apollo and Soyuz spacecraft joined up.

29

Facts about space

- There were only 10 years between Yuri Gagarin's single orbit of Earth and the launch of the first space station. Just 10 years later, the Americans launched their first shuttle.

- The first woman to travel in space was the Russian, Valentina Tereshkova, in 1963.

- The first American space station was Skylab. It weighed over 90 tonnes and was the largest object to be sent into space.

- Space is becoming crowded with bits of litter! All the bits of rockets abandoned by astronauts and satellites which no longer work are left floating in space.

Glossary

Apollo The American spacecraft which carried astronauts to the Moon.

astronaut Someone who travels in space.

atmosphere The layer of gases which surrounds some planets. On Earth it allows us to breathe.

gravity An invisible force which pulls objects together.

launch A rocket being sent into space.

mission A space visit.

orbit To travel around an object; the continuous journey of one object around another, such as the Moon around the Earth or the Earth around the Sun.

probe A robot spacecraft.

propulsion Pushing forward – the force which pushes a rocket into space.

rocket A vehicle which is pushed forward by hot gas produced inside it.

satellite An object which orbits another.

spacecraft Ships which travel through space.

stage One section of a rocket built for long flights or journeys in space.

telescope An instrument which makes objects appear larger and closer.

Index

Photographic credits:
China Great Wall Industry
Corporation/Science Photo
Library 7; Genesis Space
Photo Library 10; Robert
Harding Picture Library (Dave
Jacobs) 5; NASA 3, 9, 12,
15, 19, 27, 28; TRH Pictures
17, 20, 22, 25.